❖

Treasury of
GERMAN LOVE

❖

More *Treasury of Love*
Poems, Quotations & Proverbs available:

Treasury of French Love

Treasury of Italian Love

Treasury of Jewish Love

Treasury of Polish Love

Treasury of Roman Love

Treasury of Russian Love

Treasury of Spanish Love

Each collection also available as an Audio Book

Hippocrene Books
171 Madison Avenue
New York, NY 10016

Treasury of
GERMAN LOVE

❖

Poems, Quotations & Proverbs

In German and English

Edited by
Almut Hille

HIPPOCRENE BOOKS
New York

Contents
Poetry - p.2-76

Quotations - p.80

Proverbs - p.96

❖

GERMAN
LOVE POEMS

Johann Wolfgang von Goethe

Wenn auf beschwerlichen Reisen ein Jüngling zur Liebsten sich windet,
Hab er dies Büchlein; es ist reizend and tröstlich zugleich.
Und erwartet dereinst ein Mädchen den Liebsten, sie halte
Dieses Büchlein, und nur, kommt er, so werfe sie's weg.

If on a rough journey a young man struggles up to his love,
Let him have this small book; it's charming and comforting
    too.
And if some day a girl waits for him, let her have
This small book, and after he comes, let her throw it away.

Willst du mit reinem Gefühl der Liebe Freuden genießen,
    O laß Frechheit und Ernst ferne vom Herzen dir sein.
Die will Amorn verjagen, und *der* gedenkt ihn zu fesseln;
    Beiden das Gegenteil lächelt der schelmische Gott.

If you wish to enjoy the pure feeling of love's delight,
    Let insolence and gravity both be far from your heart.
The former will drive away Amor, the latter plans to enchain him;
    The god in his knavishness smiles at the contrast they offer.

Ha! ich kenne dich, Amor, so gut als einer! Da bringst du
 Deine Fackel, und sie leuchtet im Dunkel uns vor.
Aber du führest uns bald auf verworrene Pfade; wir brauchten
 Deine Fackel erst recht, ach! und die falsche erlischt.

Ha! I know you, Love, as well, as another; you bring
    Your torch, and it sheds its light on the shadows before us.
But you take us quickly down the tangled path; we have need for
    Your torch more than ever; ah, the faithless thing goes out.

DER ERFAHRENE
ANTWORTET BEI EINEM
GESELLSCHAFTLICHEN FRAGESPIEL

Geh den Weibern zart entgegen:
Du gewinnst sie, auf mein Wort!
Und wer rasch ist und verwegen,
Kommt vielleicht noch besser fort.
Doch wem wenig dran gelegen
Scheinet, ob er reizt und rührt,
Der beleidigt, der verführt.

THE VOICE OF EXPERIENCE

Meet women with tender bearing,
you will conquer them, I bet;
and the quick man who is daring
will perhaps do better yet;
but the man who seems uncaring
what response he may unloose
will offend and thus seduce.

NACHTGEDANKEN

Euch bedaur ich, unglücksel'ge Sterne,
Die ihr schön seid und so herrlich scheinet,
Dem bedrängten Schiffer gerne leuchtet,
Unbelohnt von Göttern und von Menschen:
Denn ihr liebt nicht, kanntet nie die Liebe!
Unaufhaltsam führen ew'ge Stunden
Eure Reihen durch den weiten Himmel.
Welche Reise habt ihr schon vollendet,
Seit ich, weilend in dem Arm der Liebsten,
Euer und der Mitternacht vergessen!

THOUGHTS BY NIGHT

You I pity, miserable stars,
that are fair and shine so splendidly,
lend your light to distressed fishermen,
unrewarded both by men and gods;
for you love not, never knew what love is!
But relentlessly eternal hours
lead your legions through the far-flung heavens.
Ah, what journey have you just completed
since I, resting in my loved one's arms,
did not even think of you at midnight.

NÄHE DES GELIEBTEN

Ich denke dein, wenn mir der Sonne Schimmer
  Vom Meere strahlt;
Ich denke dein, wenn sich des Mondes Flimmer
  In Quellen malt.

Ich sehe dich, wenn auf dem fernen Wege
  Der Staub sich hebt;
In tiefer Nacht, wenn auf dem schmalen Stege
  Der Wandrer bebt.

Ich höre dich, wenn dort mit dumpfem Rauschen
  Die Welle steigt;
Im stillen Haine geh ich oft zu lauschen,
  Wenn alles schweigt.

Ich bin bei dir, du seist auch noch so ferne,
  Du bist mir nah!
Die Sonne sinkt, bald leuchten mir die Sterne.
  O wärst du da!

NEARNESS OF HER LOVER

I think of you when the sun's glorious shimmer
    shines from the sea;
I think of you when the moon's pallid glimmer
    edges the tree.

I behold you when on the distant ridge
    The dust throws veils,
in deepest night when on the narrow bridge
    the wanderer quails.

I hear your voice when roaring billows glisten
    in thunderous riot.
In the still grove I often walk to listen
    when all is quiet.

I am with you, however far you are,
    I feel you near.
The sun goes down, soon comes the evening star.
    That you were here!

Dich sah ich, und die milde Freude
Floß von dem süßen Blick auf mich;
Ganz war mein Herz an deiner Seite
Und jeder Atemzug für dich.
Ein rosenfarbnes Frühlingswetter
Umgab das liebliche Gesicht,
Und Zärtlichkeit für mich - ihr Götter!
Ich hofft es, ich verdient es nicht!

Doch ach, schon mit der Morgensonne
Verengt der Abschied mir das Herz:
In deinen Küssen welche Wonne!
In deinem Auge welcher Schmerz!
Ich ging, du standst und sahst zur Erden,
Und sahst mir nach mit nassem Blick:
Und doch welch Glück, geliebt zu werden!
Und lieben, Götter, welch ein Glück!

I saw you, in your eye the greeting
That floods me - sweetness through and through.
For you alone my heart was beating;
For you alone the breath I drew.
Your face a glory: May and roses
Its native weather! Such concern
For me as every look discloses
I hoped for; never hoped to earn.

Damnation, dawn already! This is
Our darkest moment, parting so.
The world of rapture in your kisses!
But in your eye, the worlds of woe!
I left - your look, though lowered, stealing
Its tearful glances by the gate.
Yet being loved! It's great, the feeling!
And loving, by God above, it's great!

by John Frederick Nims

Denn die Liebe und die Thorheit / Sind Zwillingsgeschwister von alter Zeit.

Die Liebe kann wohl viel, allein die Pflicht noch mehr.

Liebe und Noth sind doch die besten Meister.

Love and folly were ever twin-sisters from old times.

Love can do much, only duty can do more.

Love and Need are always the best masters.

In einem Augenblick gewährt die Liebe,
Was Mühe kaum in langer Zeit erreicht.

Torquato Tasso, II.,

Krone des Lebens,
Glück ohne Ruh,
Liebe, bist du!

Lieder. Rastlose Liebe.

(Gerettet ist das edle Glied
Der Geisterwelt vom Bösen):
Wer immer strebend sich bemüht,
Den können wir erlösen;
Und hat an ihm die Liebe gar
Von oben teilgenommen,
Begegnet ihm die selige Schar
Mit herzlichem Wilkommen.

Faust II. V. Bergschluchten.

In one brief moment love has power to give
What anxious toil wins not in lengthen'd years.

Torquato Tasso, II., 3
Anna Swanwick

Bright crown of life,
Turbulent bliss -
Love, thou art this!

Lieder. Rastlose Liebe.

The noble Spirit now is free,
And saved from evil scheming:
Who e'er aspires unweariedly
Is not beyond redeeming.
And if he feels the grace of Love
That from On High is given,
The Blessed Hosts, that wait above,
Shall welcome him to Heaven!

Faust II. V. Bergschluchten

Ach, wer bringt die schönen Tage,
Jene Tage der ersten Liebe,
Ach, wer bringt nur eine Stunde
Jener holden Zeit zurück.

Lieder, Erster Verlust

Ein Schauspiel für Götter,
Zwei Liebende zu sehn!
Das schönste Frühlingswetter
Ist nicht so warm, so schön.

Erwin und Elmire, I, 1

Ah, who brings the happy moments,
Glorious days of sweet first love;
Who can bring back a single hour
Of that blessed time again.

Lieder, Erster Verlust

A sight for the Immortals
A happy loving pair,
The best of spring's fair weather
Is not so warm and fair.

Erwin und Elmire, I, 1

Adalbert von Chamisso

von FRAUEN, LIEBE UND LEBEN

Er, der herrlichste von allen,
Wie so milde, wie so gut!
Holde Lippen, klares Auge,
Hellen Sinn und festen Muth.

So wie dort in blauer Tiefe,
Hell und herrlich, jener Stern,
Also er an meinem Himmel
Hell und herrlich, hoch und fern.

from WOMAN'S LOVE AND LIFE

He, the best of all, the noblest,
O how gentle! O how kind!
Lips of sweetness, eyes of brightness,
Steadfast courage, lucid mind!

As on high, in Heaven's azure,
Bright and splendid, beams yon star,
Thus he in my heaven beameth,
Bright and splendid, high and far.

Friederich Rückert

Liebst du um Schönheit, o nicht mich liebe!
Liebe die Sonne, sie trägt ein goldnes Haar!
Liebst du um Jugend, o nicht mich liebe!
Liebe den Frühling, der jung ist jedes Jahr!
Liebst du um Schätze, o nicht mich liebe!
Liebe die Meerfrau, sie hat viel Perlen klar!
Liebst du um Liebe, o ja mich liebe!
Liebe mich immer, dich lieb ich immer immerdar!

Lov`st thou but beauty, O never love me!
Go, love the sunbeam, a stream with golden hair!
Lov`st thou but youthhood, O never love me!
Go love the Mayqueen, for ever young and fair!
Lov`st thou but riches, O never love me!
Go, love the mermaid, whose caverns pearls do bear!
Lov`st thou for love`s sake, then ever love me!
Love me for ever, I`ll love thee ever naught so dear!

by John Bernhoff

Franz Grillparzer

KÜß

Auf die Hände küßt die Achtung,
Freundschaft auf die offne Stirne,
Auf die Wange Wohlgefallen,
Sel'ge Liebe auf den Mund;
Aufs geschloßne Aug' die Sehnsucht,
In die hohle Hand Verlangen,
Arm und Nacken die Begierde;
Alles weitre Raserei!

A KISS

A hand is to be kissed with reverence,
The forehead—solemnly, with friendship,
The cheeks—with tender admiration,
And the lips be kissed with ardor,
While the eyes one kisses with langour,
The neck—with passionate desire,
And with a maddening delirium
All the rest is to be kissed.

by Ann Zeller

Das eben ist der Liebe Zaubermacht,
Dass sie veredelt, was ihr Hauch berührt,
Der Sonne ähnlich, deren goldner Strahl
Gewitterwolken selbst in Gold verwandelt.
Sappho, I, 5

This constitutes the witchery of love,
That she ennobles, with her touch so light,
All things below. Like from the sun, whose beam
Can turn to gold the cloud of tempest's night.

from Sappho, I, 5

Heinrich Heine

DAS FISCHERMÄDCHEN

Du schönes Fischermädchen,
treibe den Kahn an's Land;
Komm' zu mir und setze dich nieder,
wir kosen Hand in Hand.

Leg' an mein Herz dein Köpfchen
und fürchte dich nicht zu sehr;
vertrau'st du dich doch sorglos
täglich dem wilden Meer!

Mein Herz gleicht ganz dem Meere,
hat Sturm und Ebb' und Fluth,
und manche schöne Perle
in seiner Tiefe ruht.

THE FISHERMAIDEN

You lovely fishermaiden,
Bring now the boat to land:
Come here and sit beside me,
We will prattle hand in hand.

Your head lay on my bosom,
Nor be afraid of me:
Do you not trust all fearless
Daily the great wide sea?

My heart is like the sea, dear,
Has storm, and ebb, and flow,
And many purest pearl-gems
Within its dim depth glow.

by James Thomson

Ein Jüngling liebt ein Mädchen,
Die hat einen andern erwählt;
Der andre liebt eine andre,
Und hat sich mit dieser vermählt.

Das Mädchen heiratet aus Ärger
Den ersten besten Mann,
Der ihr in den Weg gelaufen;
Der Jüngling ist übel dran.

Es ist eine alte Geschichte,
Doch bleibt sie immer neu;
Und wem sie just passieret,
Dem bricht das Herz entzwei.

A young man loves a maiden,
Who loves another youth;
This other loves another,
To whom he's wed in truth.

The maiden marries in anger
The first that comes along
By chance to cross her pathway;
The young man feels this wrong.

It is an age-old story,
And yet it's always new;
The heart to whom this happens,
Will surely split in two.

by D.G.Wright

Es war ein alter König,
Sein Herz war schwer, sein Haupt war grau;
Der arme, alte König,
Er nahm eine junge Frau.

Es war ein schöner Page,
Blond war sein Haupt, leicht war sein Sinn;
Er trug die seidne Schleppe
Der jungen Königin.

Kennst du das alte Liedchen?
Es klingt so süß, es klingt so trüb!
Sie mußten beide sterben,
Sie hatten sich viel zu lieb.

There was an aged monarch,
His heart was grave, his hair was gray;
This poor old monarch married
A maid that was young and gay.

There was a handsome page-boy,
Blond was his hair, bright was his mien;
He bore the silken train
Of this so youthful queen.

You know this old, old story?
It sounds so sweet, so sad to tell!
The lovers had to perish,
They loved each other too well.

by Karl Weimar

Und wüssten's die Blumen, die kleinen,
Wie tief verwundet mein Herz,
Sie würden mit mir weinen,
Zu heilen meinen Schmerz.

Und wüssten's die Nachtigallen,
Wie ich so traurig und krank,
Sie liessen fröhlich erschallen
Erquickenden Gesang.

Und wüssten sie mein Wehe,
Die goldnen Sternelein,
Sie kämen aus ihrer Höhe,
Und sprächen Trost mir ein.

Die alle können's nicht wissen,
Nur Eine kennt meinen Schmerz:
Sie hat ja selbst zerrissen,
Zerrissen mir das Herz.

Could the little flowers divine
How deep is the wound in my heart,
Their tears they would mingle with mine
To ease of my sorrows the smart.

And did but the nightingales know
How great is my sadness and pain,
The groves and the valleys below
Would ring with their quickening strain.

The little stars golden and bright,
Knew they but my sorrow and woe,
Descending to me from the height,
Their accents of comfort would flow.

But none of them know what I've borne,
One only, she knoweth my pain.
For is it not she that hath torn,
And rent my sad heart in twain?

Warum sind denn die Rosen so blass,
O sprich, mein Lieb, warum?
Warum sind denn im grünen Gras
Die blauen Veilchen so stumm?

Warum singt denn mit so kläglichem Laut
Die Lerche in der Luft?
Warum steigt denn aus dem Balsamkraut
Hervor ein Leichenduft?

Warum scheint denn die Sonn' auf die Au'
So kalt und verdriesslich herab?
Warum ist denn die Erde so grau
Und öde wie ein Grab?

Warum bin ich selbst so krank und so trüb',
Mein liebes Liebchen, sprich?
O sprich, mein herzallerliebstes Lieb,
Warum verliesst du mich?

O wherefore are the roses so pale?
O speak, my love, say why!
And wherefore are in grassy vale
The violets silent and shy?

Why sings the lark such a querulous chant
As he soars aloft in the skies?
And wherefore from each balsamic plant
Doth the odor of death arise?

Why shines the sun o'er the plain with a ray
Of coldness, sadness and gloom?
And why is the earth so darksome and grey.
And desert as it were a tomb?

And wherefore am I so sick and depressed?
Dear maiden, tell to me!
My sweet, sweet love, my fondest, best,
Why hast thou forsaken me?

Liebste, sollst mir heute sagen:
Bist du nicht ein Traumgebild?
Wie's in schwülen Sommertagen
Aus dem Hirn des Dichters quillt?

Aber nein, ein solches Mündchen
Solcher Augen Zauberlicht,
Solch ein liebes, süßes Kindchen,
Das erschafft der Dichter nicht.

Basilisken und Vampyre,
Lindenwürm' und Ungeheu'r,
Solche schlimmer Fabeltiere,
Die erschafft des Dichters Feu'r.

Aber dich und deine Tücke,
Und dein süßes Angesicht,
Und die falschen, frommen Blicke -
Das erschaft der Dichter nicht.

Tell me, dearest maiden, tell me!
Art thou not a vision bright,
Such as, in the glow of summer,
Poets dream of with delight?

But no, no! to paint the flashes
Of thy bright bewitching eye,
Such sweet lips, so fair a maiden
Doth in vain the poet try.

Basilisks and greedy vampyres,
Monsters dread and dragons dire,
And such fearful, fabled creatures,
These breathe in the poet's fire.

But thee and thy wanton malice,
And the sweetness of thy face,
And thy looks so false, so modest,
Such no poet's pen can trace.

Hat man die Liebe durchgeliebt,
Fängt man die Freundschaft an.

Verschiedene. Angelique 8. Str. 2.

Sie liebten sich beide, doch keiner
Wollt es dem andern gestehn;
Sie sahen sich an so feindlich,
Und wollten vor Liebe vergehn.

Buch der Lieder. Die Heimkehr, 36.

Das Schweigen ist der Liebe keusche Blüte.

Letzte Gedichte, Für die Mouche, Str.

When we have lived through love's delights
With friendship we begin.

from Verschiedene. Angelique 8. Str. 2.

They loved each other, but neither
Would be the first to confess;
Like foes, they gaz'd at each other,
And would die of their love's distress.

from Buch der Lieder. Die Heimkehr, 36.

By silence is love's modest blossom cover'd.

from Letzte Gedichte, Für die Mouche, Str. 24

Nikolaus Lenau

AN DIE ENTFERNTE

Diese Rose pflück ich hier,
In der fremden Ferne;
Liebes Mädchen, dir, ach dir
Brächt ich sie so gerne!

Doch bis ich zu dir mag ziehn
Viele weite Meilen,
Ist die Rose längst dahin,
Denn die Rosen eilen.

Nie soll weiter sich ins Land
Lieb von Liebe wagen,
Als sich blühend in der Hand
Läßt die Rose tragen;

Oder als die Nachtigall
Halme bringt zum Neste,
Oder als ihr süßer Schall
Wandert mit dem Weste.

TO HER FAR AWAY

Here in foreign land this rose
I have gathered sadly
And would take this rose I chose
To you, dear girl, gladly.

But ere back to you I fly
Over hill and valley,
Wither will the rose and die;
Roses cannot dally.

Let not ever farther stray
Love from love and lover
Than a rose in bloom will stay,
In a cupped hand's cover,

Than a nesting nightingale
Roams for twigs and grasses,
Than its song down through the vale
With its west wind passes.

by Alexander Gode

KOMMEN UND SCHEIDEN

So oft sie kam, erschien mir die Gestalt
So lieblich, wie das erste Grün im Wald.

Und was sie sprach, drang mir zum Herzen ein
Süss, wie des Frühlings erstes Lied im Hain.

Und als Lebwohl sie winkte mit der Hand,
War's, ob der letzte Jugendtraum mir schwand.

ARRIVAL AND SEPARATION

Whenever she approached, her form to me appeared
As lovely as the first green in the woods.

And what she said, pierced my heart
Sweet as the spring's first song in the glade.

And when with her hand she waved farewell,
It was as if youth's final dream went from me.

Eduard Mörike

ZITRONENFALTER IM APRIL

Grausame Frühlingssonne,
Du weckst mich vor der Zeit,
Denn nur in Maienwonne
Die zarte Kost gedeiht!
Ist nicht ein liebes Mädchen hier,
Das auf der Rosenlippe mir
Ein Tröpfchen Honig beut,
So muß ich jämmerlich vergehn
Und wird der Mai mich nimmer sehn
In meinem gelben Kleid.

BRIMSTONE BUTTERFLY IN APRIL

O cruel April sunshine,
Too soon you wake me up;
I thrive but on the dainties
Of May's exchanging cup.
And if no maiden sweet there be,
Whose rosy lips will offer me
A sip of honey dew,
Then wretched must I surely die,
And May will never see me fly,
Dressed in my yellow hue.

by Geoffrey Herbert Chase

DAS VERLASSENE MÄGDLEIN

Früh, wann die Hähne krähn,
Eh' die Sternlein verschwinden,
Muß ich am Herde stehn,
Muß Feuer zünden.

Schön ist der Flamme Schein,
Es springen die Funken;
Ich schaue so drein,
In Leid versunken.

Plötzlich, da kommt es mir,
Treuloser Knabe,
Daß ich die Nacht von dir
Geträumet habe.

Träne auf Träne dann
Stürzet hernieder;
So kommt der Tag heran-
O ging er wieder!

THE FORSAKEN GIRL

Early in the starlight still,
And the cocks crowing,
I must stand at the hob,
Must get the fire going.

Sparks leap, and lovely
The flames ablaze;
Sunk in sorrow,
At them I gaze.

Suddenly then recall,
Faithless lover,
Last night I dreamed of you,
Over and over.

Tear upon tear now
Tumbling down;
So the day comes and comes-
Would it were gone.

by Christopher Middleton

So ist die Lieb! So ist die Lieb!
Mit Küssen nicht zu stillen.

Lieb' ist wie Wind,
Rasch und lebendig,
Ruhet nie,
Ewig ist sie,
Aber nicht immer beständig.

Gedichte, Lied vom Winde

Such is love. You cannot still it with kisses.

Love's like the wind,
Living and playing,
Rests never,
Lives for ever,
Yet sometimes from constancy straying.
Gedichte, Lied vom Winde

Friedrich Hebbel

ICH UND DU

Wir träumten voneinander
Und sind davon erwacht,
Wir leben, um uns zu lieben,
Und sinken zurück in die Nacht.

Du tratst aus meinem Traume,
Aus deinem trat ich hervor,
Wir sterben, wenn sich Eines
Im Andern ganz verlor.

Auf einer Lilie zittern
Zwei Tropfen, rein und rund,
Zerfließen in Eins und rollen
Hinab in des Kelches Grund.

YOU AND I

We dreamed of one another
And wakened to the light;
We live to love each other
And sink back into the night.

You stepped out of my dreaming,
Out of your dream stepped I;
If either is ever wholly
Lost in the other, we die.

Upon a lily tremble
Two clear, round drops. They kiss,
Dissolve into one, and go rolling
Into the throat's abyss.

by Calvin S. Brown

Theodor Storm

Schließe mir die Augen beide
Mit den lieben Händen zu!
Geht doch alles, was ich leide,
Unter deiner Hand zur Ruh.

Und wie leise sich der Schmerz
Well' um Welle schlafen leget,
Wie der letzte Schlag sich reget,
Füllest du mein ganzes Herz.

Both my eyes, my dearest, close
With your loving hands, I pray!
All my sufferings, all my woes,
Neath your hands are smoothed away.

Softly as the pain is stilled,
Each successive wave abates,
As the final beat pulsates,
All my heart with you is filled.

by D.G.Wright

TROST

So komme, was da kommen mag!
Solang du lebest, ist es Tag.

Und geht es in die Welt hinaus,
Wo du mir bist, bin ich zu Haus.

Ich seh dein liebes Angesicht,
Ich sehe die Schatten der Zukunft nicht.

CONSOLATION

Let come what will, let come what may!
So long you live, it is still day.

Wherever in the world I roam,
Where'er you are, for me is home.

I gaze upon your lovely face,
No shadows of the future trace.

by D.G. Wright

Leben und Liebe, - wie fliegt es vorbei!

Loving and living - how fast they flee away!

Frank Wedekind

GALATHEA

Ach, wie brenn' ich vor Verlangen,
Galathea, schönes Kind,
Dir zu küssen deine Wangen
Weil sie so entzückend sind.

Wonne die mir wiederfahre,
Dir zu küssen deine Haare...

Nimmer wehr' mir's bis ich ende,
Dir zu küssen deine Hände...

Ach, du ahnst nicht, wie ich glühe,
Dir zu küssen deine Knie...

Und was tät ich nicht, du Süße,
Dir zu küssen deine Füße...

Aber deinen Mund enthülle,
Mädchen, meinen Küssen nie,
Denn in seiner Reize Fülle,
Küßt ihn nur die Phantasie.

GALATHEA

Ah, I'm burning with desire,
Galathea, lovely child,
Just to kiss your cheeks of fire,
For they're so alluring, wild.

How I yearn for those caresses,
Just to kiss your flowering tresses...

Everymore my heart demands,
Just to kiss your graceful hands...

Ah, just see, I burn, I freeze,
Just to kiss your pretty knees...

Ah, what wouldn't I do, my sweet,
Just to kiss your dainty feet,

But to my kisses, darling maiden,
Revealed your lips shall never be,
For the fullness of their charms,
Are only found in fantasy.

Otto Julius Bierbaum

KOMM HER UND LAß DICH KÜSSEN

Die Luft ist wie voll Geigen,
Von allen Blütenzweigen
Das weiße Wunder schneit;
Der Frühling tobt im Blute,
Zu allem Übermute
Ist jetzt die allerbeste Zeit.

Komm her und laß dich küssen!
Du wirst es dulden müssen,
Daß dich mein Arm umschlingt.
Es geht durch alles Leben
Ein Pochen und ein Beben:
Das rote Blut, es singt, es singt.

COME HERE AND LET ME KISS YOU

The air is as if full of violins,
From all the flourishing branches
A white wonder pours down;
Spring rages in the blood,
This is the best time
For all kinds of merriment.

Come here and let me kiss you!
You must submit
To my arm embracing you.
Knocking and shaking
Goes through the whole life:
That is the red blood, it sings, it sings.

by Ann Zeller

Hugo von Hofmannsthal

DIE BEIDEN

Sie trug den Becher in der Hand,
- ihr Kinn und Mund glich seinem Rand -,
So leicht und sicher war ihr Gang,
Kein Tropfen aus dem Becher sprang.

So leicht und fest war seine Hand:
Er ritt auf einem jungen Pferde,
Und mit nachläßiger Gebärde
Erzwang er, daß es zitternd stand.

Jedoch, wenn er aus ihrer Hand,
Den leichten Becher nehmen sollte,
So war es beiden allzuschwer:
Denn beide bebten sie so sehr,
Dass keine Hand die andre fand
Und dunkler Wein am Boden rollte.

THE TWO

She bore the goblet in her hand -
her chin and mouth firm as its band -
her stride so weightless and so still
that not a drop would ever spill.

So weightless and so firm his hand:
he rode a young horse for his pleasure
and, looking like incarnate leisure,
compelled it; trembling it must stand.

But when he should take from her hand
the goblet that she lifted up,
the two were quivering so much
that each hand missed the other's touch,
and heavy grew the weightless cup
till dark wine rolled upon the sand.

Rainer Maria Rilke

LIEBES-LIED

Wie soll ich meine Seele halten, dass
sie nicht an deine rührt? Wie soll ich sie
hinheben über dich zu andern Dingen?
Ach, gerne möcht ich sie bei irgendwas
Verlorenem im Dunkel unterbringen
an einer fremden stillen Stelle, die
nicht weiterschwingt, wenn deine Tiefen schwingen.
Doch alles, was uns anrührt, dich und mich,
nimmt uns zusammen wie ein Bogenstrich,
der aus zwei Saiten eine Stimme zieht.
Auf welches Instrument sind wir gespannt?
Und welcher Geiger hat uns in der Hand?
O süsses Lied.

LOVE SONG

How could I keep my soul so that it might
not touch on yours? How could I elevate
it over you to reach to other things?
Oh, I would like to hide it out of sight
with something lost in endless darkenings,
in some remote, still place, so desolate
it does not sing whenever your depth sings.
Yet all that touches us, myself and you,
takes us together like a violin bow
that draws a single voice out of two strings.
Upon what instrument have we been strung?
And who is playing with us in his hand?
Sweet is the song.

Hermann Hesse

ICH LIEBE FRAUEN

Ich liebe Frauen, die vor tausend Jahren
Geliebt von Dichtern und besungen waren.

Ich liebe Städte, deren leere Mauern
Königsgeschlechter alter Zeit betrauern.

Ich liebe Städte, die erstehen werden,
Wenn niemand mehr von heute lebt auf Erden.

Ich liebe Frauen - schlanke, wunderbare,
Die ungeboren ruhn im Schoss der Jahre.

Sie werden einst mit ihrer sternebleichen
Schönheit der Schönheit meiner Träume gleichen.

I LOVE WOMEN

I love women who a thousand years ago
Were loved by poets and in songs extolled.

I love cities whose empty walls
Bemoan the ancient royal houses.

I love cities that will rise,
When no one of today is still alive on earth.

I love women-slender, wonderful,
Who rest unborn within the womb of time.

Some day they will with their starry-pale
Beauty equal the beauty of my dreams.

Albert Salus

DER GENÜGSAME LIEBHABER

Meine Freundin hat eine schwarze Katze
Mit weichem, knisterndem Sammetfell.
Und ich, ich hab' eine blitzblanke Glatze,
Blitzblank und glatt und silberhell.

Meine Freundin gehört zu den üppigen Frauen,
Sie liegt auf dem Diwan das ganze Jahr,
Beschäftigt das Fell ihrer Katze zu kraulen,
Mein Gott, ihr behagt halt das samtweiche Haar.

Und komm' ich am Abend die Freundin besuchen,
So liegt die Mieze am Schoße bei ihr,
Und nascht mit ihr von dem Honigkuchen,
Und schauert wenn ich leise ihr Haar berühr.

Und will ich mal zärtlich tun mit dem Schatze,
Und daß sie mir auch einmal "Eitschi" macht,
Dann stülp' ich die Katze auf meine Glatze,
Dann streichelt die Freundin die Katze und lacht.

THE CONTENTED SUITOR

My sweet girlfriend has a black-coated cat,
With soft fur, rustling and velvety,
And I, I have a quite shiny bald spot,
Shiny and slick and silvery.

My girlfriend's a lady of the voluptuous sort,
She lies on the sofa the whole year round,
Quite busily stroking the cat's fur for sport,
My God, how she dotes on that soft, furry mound.

And when I at evening a visit make,
Then I hear the cat on her lap loudly purr,
While nibbling with her from the honey cake,
It trembles whenever I stroke its fur.

And if I desire to caress my darling
So that she might say "kitchie koo" to me,
Then I place the pussy on my bald spot
So my girlfriend then pets it and laughs with glee.

Hans Arp

Du lächeltest,
um nicht zu weinen.
Du lächeltest,
als würden lange noch
die guten Tage scheinen.
Deine Flügel glänzten
wie junge Blätter.
Dein Gesicht
war ein weißer Stern.

Seitdem du gestorben bist,
danke ich jedem vergehenden Tag.
Jeder vergangene Tag
bringt mich dir näher.

You have smiled
so that you wouldn't cry.
You have smiled
as if bright days
would shine for a long time.
Your wings glittered
like young leaves.
Your face was like a white star.

Since you have died,
I thank every passing day.
Every passing day
brings me closer to you.

by Ann Zeller

Bertolt Brecht

ERINNERUNG AN DIE MARIE A.

An jenem Tag im blauen Mond September
Still unter einem jungen Pflaumenbaum
Da hielt ich sie, die stille bleiche Liebe
In meinem Arm wie einen holden Traum.
Und über uns im schönen Sommerhimmel
War eine Wolke, die ich flüchtig sah.
Sie war sehr weiss und ungeheuer oben,
Und als ich aufsah, war sie nimmer da.

Seit jenem Tag sind viele, viele Monde
Geschwommen still hinunter und vorbei
Die Pflaumenbäume sind wohl abgehauen
Und fragst du mich, was mit der Liebe sei?
So sag ich dir: ich kann mich nicht erinnern.
Und doch, gewiss, ich weiss schon, was du meinst.
Doch ihr Gesicht, das weiss ich wirklich nimmer
Ich weiss nur mehr: Ich küsste es dereinst.

Und auch den Kuss, ich hätt' ihn längst vergessen
Wenn nicht die Wolke da gewesen wär.
Die weiss ich noch und werd ich immer wissen
Sie war sehr weiss und kam von oben her.
Die Pflaumenbäume blühn vielleicht noch immer.
Und jene Frau hat jetzt vielleicht das siebte Kind.
Doch jene Wolke blühte nur Minuten
Und als ich aufsah, schwand sie schon im Wind.

IN MEMORY OF MARIE A.

One day in the blue month of September
Silently I held her under a young plum tree,
I held her there, my pale and silent loved one,
And like a gentle dream within my arms was she.
And over us in the fair summer heavens
Was a cloud that fleetingly I saw,
Very white and terribly far above us,
And as I looked up it was there no more.

Since that day so many, many months
Have silently swum by and are no more.
No doubt the plum trees have been all cut down.
And if you ask me what became of her
I'll tell you truly that I don't remember.
I know already why you ask me this,
And yet her face I really have forgotten,
I know no more of it than that one kiss.

Even the kiss I should have quite forgotten
If there had been no cloud there, long ago.
I see it still and I shall always see it
For it was white and drifted down like snow.
Perhaps the plum trees bear their yearly blossoms,
Perhaps the woman has her seventh child,
And yet that cloud bloomed only for a minute
And as I looked up vanished in the wind.

Mascha Kaleko

GROßSTADTLIEBE

Man lernt sich irgendwo ganz flüchtig kennen
Und gibt sich irgendwann ein Rendezvous,
Ein Irgendwas,-'s ist nicht genau zu nennen-
Verführt dazu, sich gar nicht mehr zu trennen.
Beim zweiten Himbeereis sagt man sich "du."

Man hat sich lieb und ahnt im Grau der Tage
Das Leuchten froher Abendstunden schon.
Man teilt die Alltagssorgen und die Plage,
Man teilt die Freuden der Gehaltszulage,
...Das übrige besorgt das Telephon.

Man trifft sich im Gewühl der Großstadstraßen.
Zu Hause geht es nicht. Man wohnt möbliert.
-Durch das Gewirr von Lärm und Autorasen,
-Vorbei am Klatsch der Tanten und der Basen
Geht man zu zweien still und unberührt.

Man küßt sich dann und wann auf stillen Bänken,
-Beziehungsweise auf dem Paddelboot.
Erotik muß auf Sonntag sich beschränken.
...Wer denkt daran, an später noch zu denken?
Man spricht konkret und wird nur selten rot.

Man schenkt sich keine Rosen und Narzissen,
Und schickt auch keinen Pagen sich ins Haus.
-Hat man genug von Weekendfahrt und Küssen,
Läßt man's einander durch die Reichspost wissen
Per Stenographenschrift ein Wörtchen: "aus"!

LOVE IN THE CITY

Somewhere you meet each other-fleeting-
And sometimes there's a rendezvous.
A something, -it's not worth repeating-
Tempts you to prolong the meeting.
With the second sundae you say "du."

You like each other and anticipate by day
The promise of a night not spent alone.
You'll share the daily worries and dismays,
You'll share the joys of a raise in pay,
...The rest is done by telephone.

In the city's tumult you both meet.
Not at home. You live in a room in an apartment.
-Through the confusion, noise, cars on the street,
-Past the gossiping women and girls on the beat,
you go with each other, quiet, confident.

You kiss on a bench along the way,
-Or on a paddle-boat instead.
Eros must be limited to Sundays.
-You think of now-and come what may!
You speak bluntly and do not turn red.

You don't give each other narcissi or roses,
And you don't communicate by servant:
When weekend kisses cease to engross,
Then you send a letter via Federal Post:
"It's over!" written down in shorthand.

$\qquad\qquad\qquad\qquad$ *by S.L. Cocalis*

Zitate

Kein Feuer, keine Kohle kann brennen so heiss,
Als heimliche Liebe, von der niemand nichts weiss!
Heimliche Liebe. Volkslied

O! Wer kann die Wunderwerke der Liebe genug erheben?
Christian Ewald von Kleist, (1715-1759)

Eine ward herrlicher vor allen andern!
Eine ward Königin der andern alle!
Die Liebe.

Friedrich Gottlieb Klopstock (1724-1803)

Quotations

No fire, no coal burns with so fierce a glow
As secret love, of which no man doth know.
Heimliche Liebe. Volkslied

O who can the wondrous works of love enough extoll?
Christian Ewald von Kleist, (1715-1759)

One was more glorious far than all the others.
One was the exalted queen o'er the rest, 'twas love.
Friedrich Gottlieb Klopstock (1724-1803)

Denn ohne Lieb' und ohne Wein,
Sprich, Mensch, was bleibst du noch? - Ein Stein.
Gottfried Ephraim Lessing (1729-1781)

Gleichheit ist immer das festeste Band der Liebe.
Gottfried Ephraim Lessing,
Minna von Barnhelm, V. 8

Es ist ein holder, freundlicher Gedanke,
Dass über uns, in unermessnen Höhn,
Der Liebe Kranz aus funkelnden Gestirnen,
Da wir erst wurden, schon geflochten war.
Friedrich Schiller, Die Piccolomini, III, 4

For without love, or wine, now own!
What wouldst thou be, O man? - A stone.
Gottfried Ephraim Lessing (1729-1781)

Equality is always the strongest tie of love.
Gottfried Ephraim Lessing
Minna von Barnhelm, V. 8

It is a gentle and affectionate thought,
That in immeasurable heights above us,
At our birth, the wreath of love was woven,
With sparkling stars for flowers.
Friedrich Schiller, (1759-1805) Die
Piccolomini, III, 4
Transl. S.T. Coleridge

Gesang und Liebe in schönem Verein,
Sie erhalten dem Leben den Jugendschein.
Friedrich Schiller, Gedichte. Die vier Weltalter

Kein Kaiser hat dem Herzen vorzuschreiben.ller, Gedichte.
Die vier Weltalter

Friedrich Schiller. Wallenstein's Tod, II., 7.

Selig durch die Liebe
Götter - durch die Liebe
Menschen Göttern gleich!
Liebe macht den Himmel
Himmlischer - die Erde
Zu dem Himmelreich.
Friedrich Schiller. Gedichte. Triumph der Liebe.

Ah, song and love in joy together blending,
Preserve for life youth's glory without ending.
> *Friedrich Schiller, Gedichte. Die vier Weltalter*

No emperor has power to prescribe
Laws for the heart.
> *Friedrich Schiller. Wallenstein's Tod, II., 7.*

By love are blest the Gods on high,
Frail man becomes a Deity
When Love to him is given;
'Tis love that makes the Heavens shine
With hues more radiant, more divine,
And turns dull Earth to Heaven!
> *Friedrich Schiller. Gedichte. Triumph der Liebe.*

Die Lieb' ist der schönste der Triebe.
Aber dann liebt auch mit weiserer Liebe
alles, was edel und schön ist und gut.
Johann Gaudenz von Salis (1762-1834)

Ist nicht heilig mein Herz, schöneren Lebens voll
Seit ich liebe?
Friedrich Hölderlin (1770-1843)

Lieben is tiefes Schmerzen.
Justinus Kerner (1786-1862)

O for love is the sweetest of feelings.
Learn then to love, with a love that is wiser,
All that is noble, exalted, and good.
Johann Gaudenz von Salis (1762-1834)

Has my heart not become sacred and filled with life
Since I've loved?
Friedrich Hölderlin (1770-1843)

Love is deepest aching.
Justinus Kerner (1786-1862)

Jede Trennung gibt einen Vorgeschmack des Todes - und
jedes Wiedersehen einen Vorgeschmack der Auferstehung.
Arthur Schopenhauer (1788-1860)

Die Liebe hat kein Mass der Zeit; sie keimt
Und blüht und reift in einer schönen Stunde.
Theodor Körner (1791-1813) Toni, II.,2.

Die Liebe scheint der zarteste der Triebe,
Das wissen selbst die Blinden und die Tauben,
Ich aber weiss, was wen'ge Menschen glauben,
Dass wahre Freundschaft zarter ist als Liebe.
August v. Platen, (1796-1835) Sonnette, 70

Every parting is a foretaste of death, and every reunion a foretaste of resurrection.
Arthur Schopenhauer (1788-1860)

Love hath no measurement in time; it buds
And blooms and ripens in one glowing hour.
Theodor Körner (1791-1813) Toni, II.,2.

Love seems, 'tis true, of impulses most tender,
Even the blind and deaf will tell us so:
Yet, what but few believe, I claim to know—
That truest friendship greater charm can render.
August von Platen (1796-1835)
Sonnette, 70

Steh ich in finstrer Mitternacht
So einsam auf der stillen Wacht,
So denk ich an mein fernes Lieb,
Ob mir's auch treu und hold verblieb.

Wilhelm Hauff.(1802-1827)
Kriegs und Volkslieder. Soldatenliebe.

Liebe bleibt die goldne Leiter,
Drauf das Herz zum Himmel steigt.

Emanuel Geibel. (1815-1884)
Lieder als Intermezzo, I.

When in the silent midnight hour
I stand upon my watch alone -
I wonder if my distant love
Is true and faithful - still my own.

Wilhelm Hauff (1802-1827).
Kriegs und Volkslieder. Soldatenliebe.

Love is e'er the golden ladder
On which the heart to Heaven mounts.

Emanuel Geibel (1815-1884).
Lieder als Intermezzo, I.

Das höchste Glück hat keine Lieder,
Der Liebe Lust ist still und mild,
Ein Kuß, ein Blicken hin und wieder,
Und alle Sehnsucht ist gestillt.

Emanuel Geibel, Jugendgedichte,
Lieder als Intermezzo, XXII, Str. 3

Das Herz bedarf des Überflusses.
Genug kann nie und nimmermehr genügen.

Konrad Ferdinand Meyer (1825-1898)

True joy doth need no song to praise it,
Silence for love's delight is best;
A kiss, a shy glance, then another
And all our longing is at rest.
> *Emanuel Geibel, Jugendgedichte,*
> *Lieder als Intermezzo, XXII, Str. 3*

The heart needs its surfeit of abundance.
Enough can never be enough again.
> *Konrad Ferdinand Meyer (1825-1898)*

Doch alle Lust will Ewigkeit - ,
Will tiefe, tiefe Ewigkeit!

Friedrich Nietzsche (1844-1900)

Die Liebe bringt die hohen und verborgenen Eigenschaften
eines Liebenden ans Licht, sein Seltenes, Ausnahmsweises:
insofern tuscht sie leicht über das, was die Regel an ihm
ist.

Friedrich Nietzsche

But every Joy wants everlastingness -
Wants deeper, deeper everlastingness!
Friedrich Nietzsche (1844-1900)

Love brings to light the noble and hidden qualities of a lover - his rare and exceptional traits: to that extent it conceals his usual character.
Friedrich Nietzsche

Sprichwörter

Lieb' ist Leides Anfang.

Die Liebe aus der Ferne bleibt am längsten warm.

Die Liebe geht durch den Magen.

Proverbs

Love is the beginning of sorrow.

Love at a distance stays warm the longest. *(lit.)*.
Absence makes the heart grow fonder.

Love goes through the stomach. *(lit.)*.
The way to a man's heart is through the stomach.

Alte Liebe rostet nicht.

Das Feuer der großen Liebe auf den ersten Blick ist bereits beim zweiten im Verlöschen.

Es war Liebe auf den ersten Blick. Nach der Hochzeit stellten beide fest, daß er kurzsichtig und sie weitsichtig war.

Old love does not rust. *(lit.)*.
   True love never grows old.

Love at first sight is often extinguished by the second.

It was love at first sight. After the wedding it turned out
that he was shortsighted and she was farsighted.

Liebe auf den ersten Blick ist die am weitesten
verbreitete Augenkrankheit.

Liebe macht blind. Der Liebende sieht mehr als da ist.

Liebe macht blind, darum tasten sich Verliebte ab.

Love at first sight is the most common eye disease.

Love is blinding. Lovers see more than there is.

Love is blinding. That is why lovers like to touch.

Kluge Frauen lieben dumme Männer.

Liebe ohne Gegenliebe ist eine Frage ohne Antwort.

Liebe muss Zank haben.

Smart women love foolish men.

Love without reciprocity is a question without an answer.

Love needs quarrel.

Gezwungene Liebe und gemalte Wangen dauern nicht.

Stroh in Schuhen und Lieb in Herzen gucken überall heraus.

Wer aus Liebe heiratet, hat gute Nächte und üble Tage.

Forced love and painted cheeks don't last.

Straw in your shoe and love in your heart will always show.

Who weds for love, has good nights and bad days.

Wo man Liebe sät, da wächst Freude.

Liebe erfüllt die Welt und mehrt den Himmel.

Der Liebe Wunden kann nur heilen, der sie schlug.

Where you sow love, joy grows.

Love fills the world and multiplies heaven.

The lover who hurts is the only one who can heal.

Liebe macht Gegenliebe.

Die Augen Sind der Liebe Tür.

Love creates love in response.

The eyes are the door of love.

INDEX

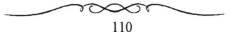